BODY IMAGE

BECAUSE ALL BODIES ARE GREAT BODIES

Tierra Hohn ▪ Illustrated by Marne Grahlman

James Lorimer & Company Ltd., Publishers
Toronto

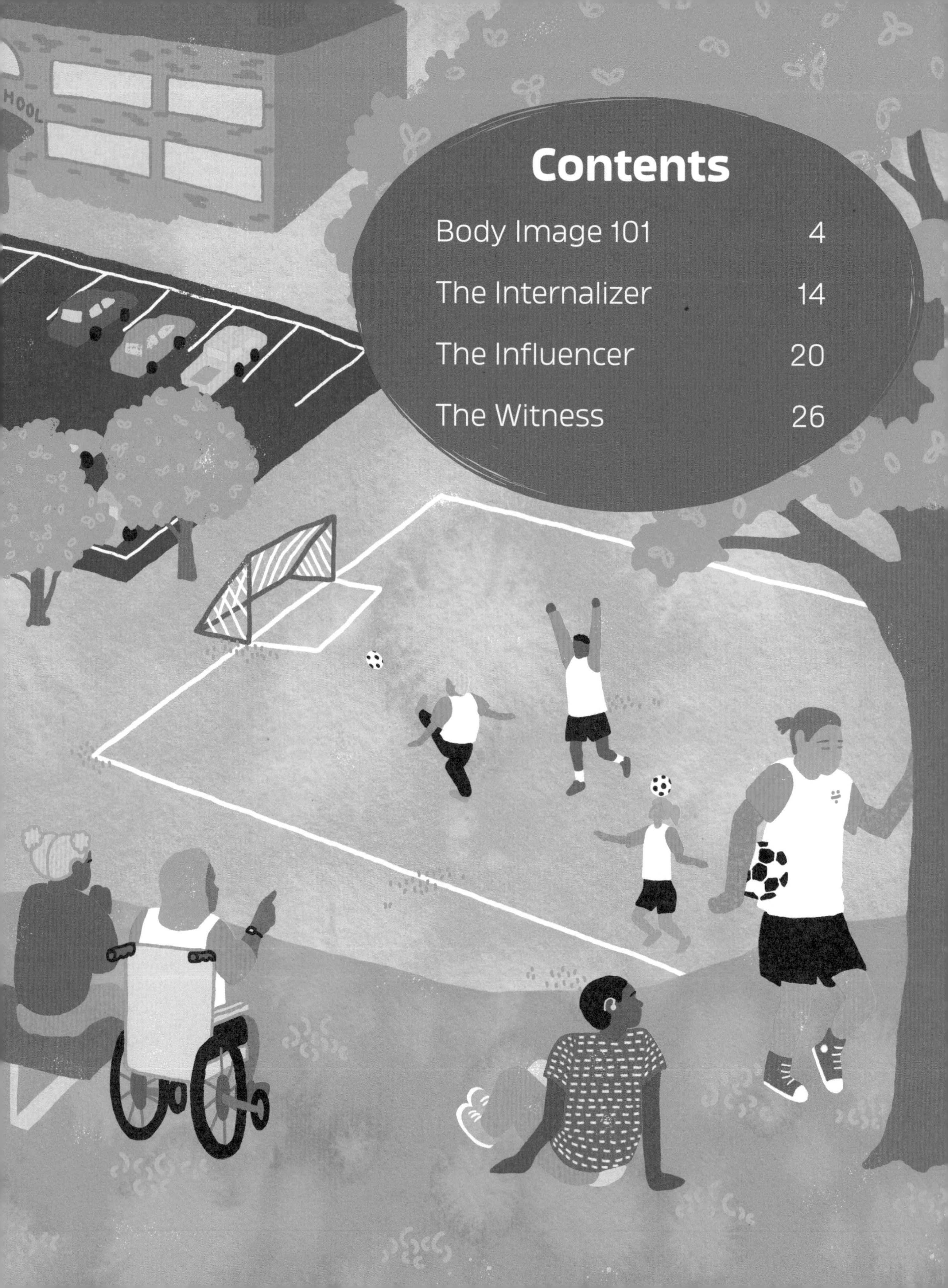
HOOL

Contents

What is everyone fussing about?

It's the first soccer practice of the school year. You've been working on your skills all summer, and it shows. But your teammates are all standing around Chris. Over the summer Chris got taller and became buff.

"Chris, you look jacked!"

"Check out those arms."

"I bet you'll be a real striker now, Chris!"

You can't believe it when Samiya, the most popular girl at school, makes a big fuss over Chris's new body. She used to taunt him for being skinny, but now she is looking at him like he's a superhero.

Why is everyone more focused on what Chris looks like than on how he plays?

After practice, Samiya asks you, "Did you even work out this summer? You still look like a string bean!" Then she laughs.

How we feel about our bodies can affect how we feel about ourselves.

Our body image can also affect how we interact with the world around us, and that can cause conflict. In this book, we'll look at conflicts caused by body image. You'll learn ways to improve your own body image and recognize qualities within yourself and others that have nothing to do with appearance.

WHAT IS BODY IMAGE?

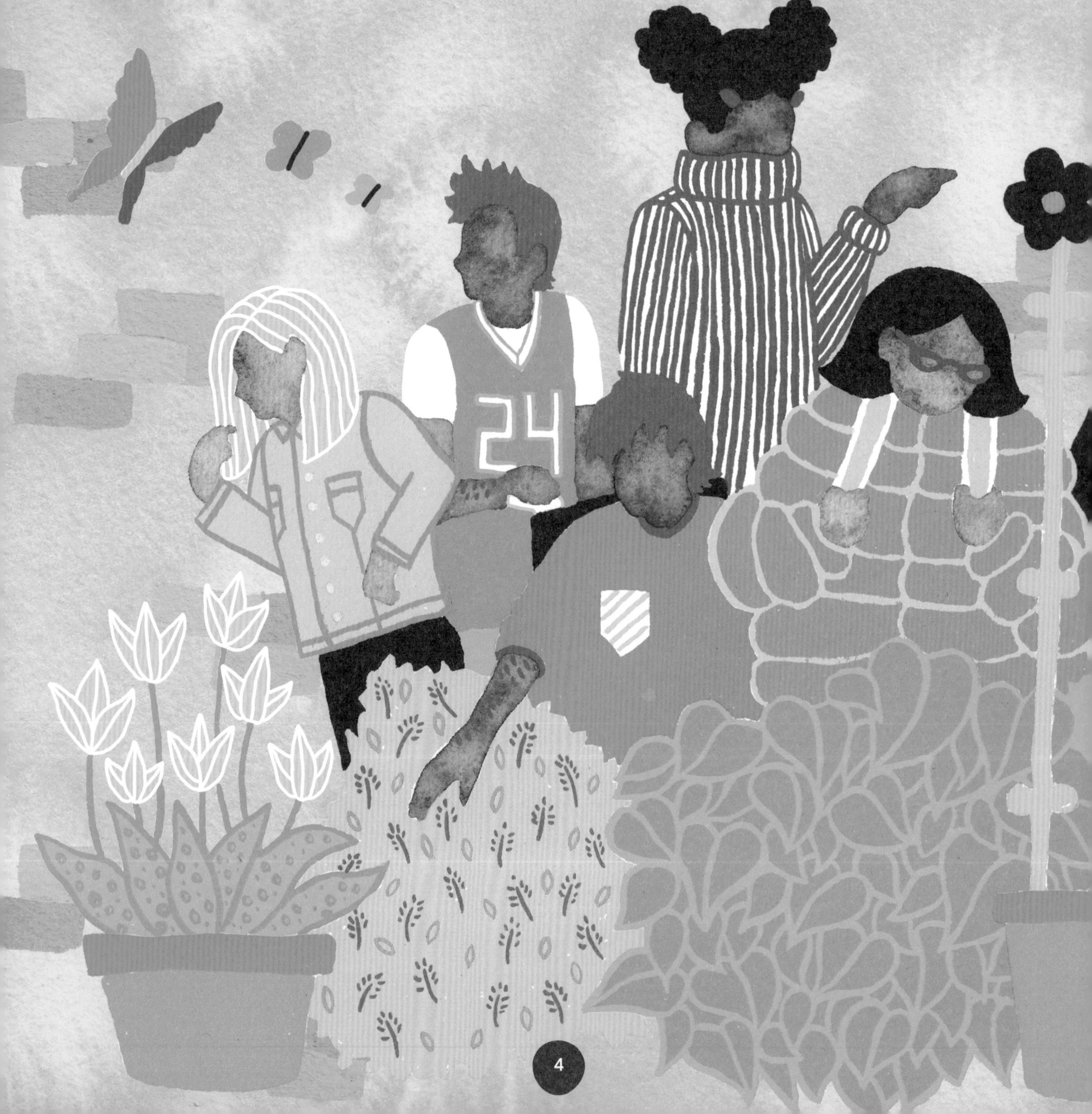
24

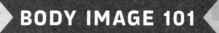

Body image is made up of the thoughts and beliefs we hold about our bodies.

This can include things like:

- Weight

- Height

- Shape/Size

- Hair

- Skin

- Other physical features

How you see your body affects how you see yourself. So, body image is also:

- How we think others perceive our appearance.

- Connected to our self-esteem.

- Influenced by the people and media around us.

- Thoughts and beliefs that can affect our physical and mental health.

Our bodies are more than just a collection of physical parts. We live in our bodies, and as they change, so does the way we feel about them.

OUR BODY IMAGE CAN BE INFLUENCED BY...

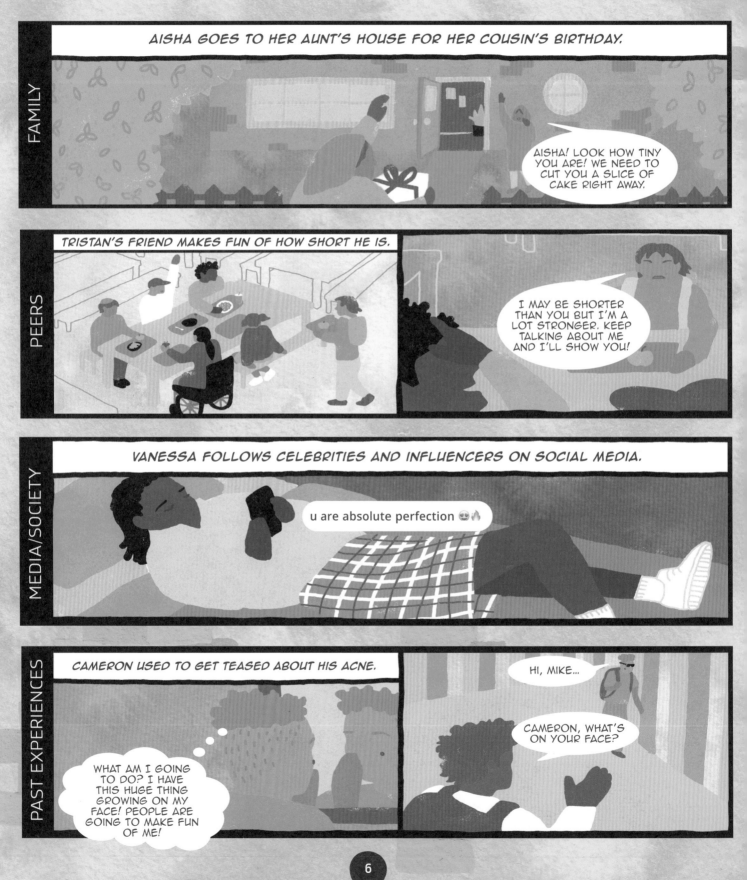

FAMILY

AISHA GOES TO HER AUNT'S HOUSE FOR HER COUSIN'S BIRTHDAY.

AISHA! LOOK HOW TINY YOU ARE! WE NEED TO CUT YOU A SLICE OF CAKE RIGHT AWAY.

PEERS

TRISTAN'S FRIEND MAKES FUN OF HOW SHORT HE IS.

I MAY BE SHORTER THAN YOU BUT I'M A LOT STRONGER. KEEP TALKING ABOUT ME AND I'LL SHOW YOU!

MEDIA/SOCIETY

VANESSA FOLLOWS CELEBRITIES AND INFLUENCERS ON SOCIAL MEDIA.

u are absolute perfection 🥺🔥

PAST EXPERIENCES

CAMERON USED TO GET TEASED ABOUT HIS ACNE.

WHAT AM I GOING TO DO? I HAVE THIS HUGE THING GROWING ON MY FACE! PEOPLE ARE GOING TO MAKE FUN OF ME!

HI, MIKE...

CAMERON, WHAT'S ON YOUR FACE?

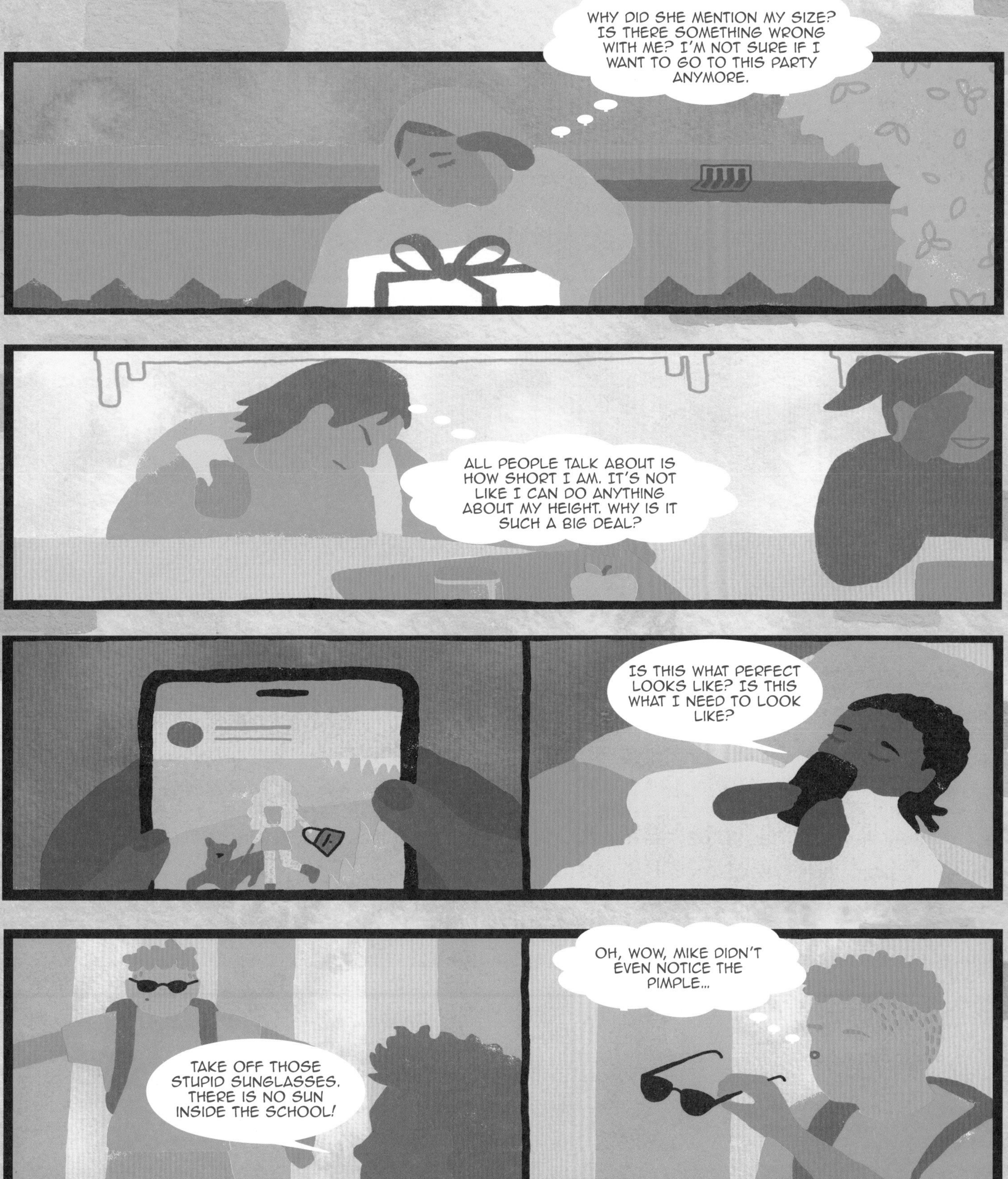
WHY DID SHE MENTION MY SIZE? IS THERE SOMETHING WRONG WITH ME? I'M NOT SURE IF I WANT TO GO TO THIS PARTY ANYMORE.
ALL PEOPLE TALK ABOUT IS HOW SHORT I AM. IT'S NOT LIKE I CAN DO ANYTHING ABOUT MY HEIGHT. WHY IS IT SUCH A BIG DEAL?
IS THIS WHAT PERFECT LOOKS LIKE? IS THIS WHAT I NEED TO LOOK LIKE?
TAKE OFF THOSE STUPID SUNGLASSES. THERE IS NO SUN INSIDE THE SCHOOL!
OH, WOW, MIKE DIDN'T EVEN NOTICE THE PIMPLE...

WHERE ON THE SCALE IS BODY IMAGE?

Body image can be an issue for some people and not for others. It's not always negative (judging ourselves as not good enough). It can also be positive (feeling good and comfortable in our own skin) or neutral (focusing less on what our bodies look like and more on what they allow us to do). Read the following scenarios and decide if each is describing a POSITIVE, NEGATIVE, or NEUTRAL body image scenario.

1. Terrance doesn't want to take off his shirt to swim because he's afraid of his body being judged.

Negative. Negative body image can have an impact on our actions. It can result in wanting to avoid people, places, or activities that we usually enjoy.

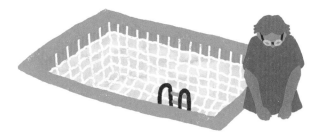

2. Cassandra doesn't like the gap between her teeth. Instead, she focuses on how her whole face lights up when she smiles.

Neutral. It would be great if we loved all parts of ourselves, but that may not always be possible. At the very least, we can try to accept ourselves.

3. Ahmad may not like every part of his body, but that doesn't mean he puts himself down. Instead he dresses in a way that reflects his personality.

Neutral. Self-talk matters. If we speak negatively about ourselves, we might begin to believe it. Say something positive about yourself the next time you stand in front of a mirror.

4. Alex has beautiful natural hair. But she wears extensions because she does not want others to ask questions or touch her real hair.

Negative. Hair is a wonderful way to express ourselves and to try out new looks. But it can be exhausting trying to please others, and it is not our job to make sure that others like the way we look.

5. Michael doesn't enjoy exercising several times a day, but he does it because he thinks it is the only way to be healthy.

Negative. Exercise is not the only way to be healthy. In fact, too much exercise can be harmful. Bodies also require rest and nutrients to be strong.

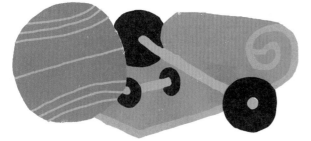

6. Fatima always used to cover her scars. Over time, she realized that her scars were a reminder of her being a survivor of a car accident, so she stopped covering them up.

Positive. We all have parts of ourselves that might make us feel uncomfortable, but we should never be ashamed of ourselves or what we have been through.

7. Amanda is the last girl in her grade to develop breasts. It makes her feel really out of place that her body does not look like her friends'.

Negative. Everyone's body is different and develops at a different rate. These differences make us unique.

8. Tiana was told by her coach to lose weight to improve her endurance. Instead, she worked harder on her technique and ended up winning most of her races.

Positive. Improving a skill requires practice, not weight loss. Losing weight is not always the answer.

9. Maya's role model has dark skin, which makes Maya feel that her own dark skin is beautiful, too.

Positive. Having a role model is important, especially if that role model looks like us! This can help to inspire and influence us in many great ways.

10. Carlos gets his weight checked every few months. His weight has gone up and down five to ten pounds over time, and he is fine with that.

Neutral. A person's weight is constantly changing, even throughout the day. Instead of focusing on the number on the scale, we could focus on taking care of ourselves, inside and out.

YOU ASKED...

Q: I was born with only one arm. I have learned how to do many different things with the arm that I have — there really isn't much that I can't do! Having one arm does not bother me, but the reaction I get from other people does. When I'm in public, I see people staring at me. It makes me feel so uncomfortable, and sometimes I try to hide my body by wearing oversized shirts. What can I do to feel more comfortable?

– Arm Cover

A: Being stared at sucks. People might be looking because they are curious — not judging — but it still feels weird. Remember that you can't control what other people do, but you can decide how you respond. Try some positive self-talk — say things like "I am unique" and "I am enough." And don't cover yourself up if you do not want to, because you are amazing exactly as you are!

Q: Lately my brother has been working out and drinking protein shakes non-stop. When I asked him about it, he told me that he was tired of being skinny and not being noticed by girls at his school. He wants to be buff like the popular guys.

– Don't Need a Different Brother

A: It is normal to want to fit in or be liked by others, but there is no need to change our appearance in order to do so. There is no rule that says that boys need to be muscular. We are all unique in the way we look, the way we think, and in the way we see the world. Ultimately, people will like you for being yourself. The next time you speak with your brother, remind him of his other great qualities.

Q: I've always been in a bigger body. It's just the way that I was made. I never had problems with how I looked until I started middle school this year and other kids started making fun of my appearance. I often get stared at and I hear laughter when I walk down the hallway. Recently, someone called me "fatty." Why do people feel the need to point out when someone might look different?

– Fat Is Where It's At

A: Everyone is allowed to take up space. Your size might make others uncomfortable, but that is their issue, not yours. Their teasing might come from the fact that they are insecure about aspects of their own appearance. Try reclaiming the word "fat." It is not a bad word, despite what others might say. And it has nothing to do with who you are inside. If you feel comfortable in your skin, then that is the only thing that matters.

MYTHS

All people who have negative body image get eating disorders.

Although negative body image is a risk factor for eating disorders, not everyone who has negative body image will develop an eating disorder.

Body image is all about our shape.

Body image can deal with weight, height, shape, size and other physical features, like hair, nose, and ears. It also includes our thoughts and feelings towards these parts of ourselves.

How I view my body is exactly how others view my body.

We can be our biggest critics. Often what we might consider as flaws are not seen the same way by others.

If you have negative body image now, you'll always struggle with it.

It is possible to get to a point where you can accept or even love your body. It does not happen overnight, but it can happen over time.

Plastic surgery and/or weight loss can fix how I feel about my body.

Body image is what we feel internally. Plastic surgery and weight loss can alter our physical appearance, but it cannot fix negative self-image.

Only some groups of people can struggle with their body image.

Body image is universal; everyone has it and anyone can struggle with their body image.

Strong men do not have body image issues.

Body image is not an issue that just affects women, it can affect anyone. Struggling with your body image does not make someone weak.

DID YOU KNOW?

- You cannot tell if someone is healthy or not based on their size alone.
- In Tonga and Mauritania, bigger women are a sign of beauty, wealth, and prestige.

- During the Victorian era, some women wore corsets and crinolines to mould their bodies into an hourglass shape. This caused many health complications.

ARE YOU AN INTERNALIZER?

You never feel like you measure up, whether it be your height, hair, skin, weight, facial features, or physique. You are always comparing how you look to others or staring in the mirror to find ways to look better. When people tease you, you sometimes wish you could change how you look. When you are out in public, you may feel invisible. At times you like it that way — if no one notices you, then no one can judge how you look. You often wonder: if you changed your appearance, would it make you feel happier with your body?

DOs & DON'Ts

✓ Do make time to take care of your body by doing things you enjoy.

✓ Do recognize that you are more than just your body.

✓ Do show gratitude to your body for what it enables you to do.

✓ Do remember that you are enough.

✓ Do challenge negative thoughts that come up about your body.

✓ Do celebrate yourself and others whenever possible.

✗ Don't get stuck trying to look or be perfect.

✗ Don't depend on validation from others to build your own body image.

✗ Don't measure your worth based on physical attributes or a number on the scale.

✗ Don't compare your body to others' bodies.

✗ Don't expect your body to always stay the same.

✗ Don't follow social media accounts that do not make you feel good.

WHAT'S YOUR GO-TO?

When someone judges you for your appearance, how does that make you feel? How do you react? You can REJECT YOUR BODY and criticize how you look. You can ACCEPT YOUR BODY and choose not to buy into their judgement. Or you can LOVE YOUR BODY and embrace who you are and remind yourself that you don't have to change. How will you respond to this quiz?

REJECT

ACCEPT

LOVE

1. Your friend posts a picture of you online and you don't like how you look in it. What do you do?

Reject: Comment on the picture, saying, "Ew, I look ugly."

Accept: Remind yourself that you are worth more than just a photo.

Love: Make peace with how you look and find the parts of the photo that you do like — for example, your smile.

2. During the holidays, a family member tells you that they think you should lose some weight. What do you do?

Reject: Take their comment as the truth and call yourself names because of it.

Accept: Ignore what that relative said. Their opinion has nothing to do with you.

Love: Remind yourself that, despite what others think, you are fine just as you are.

3. You get a last-minute call from your friend, who asks you to go to the movies. She tells you not to embarrass her by wearing baggy clothes. What do you do?

Reject: Spend a long time getting ready and end up wearing revealing clothes that you are not comfortable in.

Accept: Remind your friend that you can wear whatever you want.

Love: Wear something that you feel comfortable in, even if your friend might not approve.

4. You're watching TV with a boy that you like. When he sees a new character on the show, he jokingly asks why you can't look more like that character. What do you do?

Reject: Tear yourself apart because you think that the character on the show is way more attractive and therefore better than you.

Accept: Say you think you're great just as you are.

Love: Agree that the character is good-looking, but recognize that it does not take away from your own beauty.

5. Your mom takes you to the store to buy some new pants because your old ones no longer fit you. What do you do?

Reject: Criticize yourself because your pants no longer fit and you think you've gained weight.

Accept: Recognize that there are some changes happening to your body and be excited to get some new clothes.

Love: Remind yourself that you are still growing and it is normal for your body to change.

6. Your older cousin has been talking non-stop about a new diet they just started. They suggest that you start following it, too. What do you do?

Reject: Start to worry that you need to lose weight and ask your cousin to send you more information.

Accept: Realize that what your older cousin chooses to do or thinks about your weight has nothing to do with you.

Love: Tell your cousin that you do not need to go on a diet because you do not need to alter any part of yourself.

7. You try out for the school play, but are told you are not a good fit for the role you want. What do you do?

Reject: Compare your appearance with the person who got the role and tell yourself that you are not good enough.

Accept: Recognize that you tried your best and that is all that matters.

Love: Congratulate the person who got the role and tell yourself that there will be other roles in the future.

8. You come across a weight-loss blog. There are lots of mean comments on the "before" pictures. What do you do?

Reject: Internalize the ad and think that it is meant for you.

Accept: Leave the website and keep scrolling through your social media.

Love: Think critically about the messages you see. Remind yourself that ads are created to persuade our thinking and that you refuse to buy into it.

9. Your family plans a day trip to the water park, but you do not like how you look in a swimsuit. Your dad says you have to come. What do you do?

Reject: Make up an excuse to get out of going to the waterpark.

Accept: Go to the waterpark even though you don't feel comfortable.

Love: Go to the waterpark and allow yourself to have fun with your family without worrying about what you look like.

10. Your friend says you've been avoiding them and asks you to go on a bike ride after school. Lately you have been feeling self-conscious about how you look, so you don't really want to go. What do you do?

Reject: Make up an excuse and tell your friend you can't go.

Accept: Remind yourself that your body enables you to do activities that you enjoy such as bike riding.

Love: Go on the bike ride and have some fun spending time with your friend

FEEL LIKE YOUR INSIDE DOESN'T MATCH YOUR OUTSIDE?

Here are some things you can do:

Start by checking in with yourself. What do you feel when you think about how you look? Where do you feel these emotions in your body? How long have you had these feelings? Who can you talk to about how you're feeling? This could include a parent or guardian, a teacher, a helpline, or a counsellor.

Be aware that many images and messages in the media — including social media — are created to make us react in certain ways (that's called "curated"). They can be inaccurate or downright fake. Unfollow media that does not make you feel great about yourself. Don't be afraid to report content that is harmful to yourself or others.

Be grateful for what you have. Our bodies allow us to do many amazing things. During times when you're not feeling the greatest about your body, think about five things that your body allows you to do. For example, your stomach allows you to digest the food you eat, fueling you with energy to do the activities you love.

Remind yourself that you are more than what you look like. Write yourself a list of ten things you are good at and do not involve your physical appearance. For example: I am good at science; I am good at cooking; I am a good friend. Keep this list close to you for whenever you need to be reminded.

GENDER AND BODY IMAGE

Do you think you know how a girl should look and act? What about a boy? What about someone who does not identify as either? Gender roles are ideas of how people should act, look, speak, and dress based on their assigned sex. Think about some examples, like *girls care more about how they look* and *boys don't worry about their weight*. One problem is that these ideas are not inclusive of transgender or gender non-binary people. Another is that family, friends, environment, and media can reinforce gender roles, making them gender stereotypes — judgements or biases based on assigned sex. Gender stereotypes about physical appearance can lead to standards and ideals, like boys are to be muscular and tall, and girls are to be thin with long hair. These judgements and standards affect the way we see and treat others and ourselves.

Whether we realize it or not, gender expectations influence us all and create pressure to conform to unnecessary and unrealistic standards. Trying to live up to these ideas can put our physical and mental health at risk of a number of things, including eating disorders, depression, anxiety, and suicidal thoughts. These can also lead to harmful choices like dieting, substance abuse, and social isolation.

Gender expectations can get in our way of being our true, authentic selves, but they don't have to. We are all allowed to be who we are without buying into how society thinks we should be. There are ways we can resist gender expectations:

- Pay attention to the messages we receive and be critical about them.
- Think before we speak about others and don't reinforce stereotypes.
- Fill ourselves up with things we enjoy and that allow us to be ourselves.

DID YOU KNOW?

- 43% of girls and 27% of boys aged 11–15 years old in Canada feel dissatisfied with their bodies.

- Transgender people have a higher risk of developing an eating disorder at some point in their lives than others.

- Around 20% of people who receive cosmetic surgery are men.

ARE YOU AN INFLUENCER?

Whether you work hard at looking your best or were just born looking great, you know what standard everyone should be aiming for.

Do your peers want to look like you? Act like you? Dress like you? Or just care what you think? If you answered yes to any of these, then you have influence.

So how do you use your influence? Instead of changing yourself or others, have you thought about changing the standard? Have you considered using your influence to help others feel great?

YOU ASKED...

Q: My friend and I are planning a party at my house. I put them in charge of the invitation list. Yesterday we went through the list and everyone in our class was invited except for two people. When I asked my friend why, they said that there wouldn't be enough space for them because of their large size. I can't help but think this might be unfair. What should I do?

— **Party Person**

A: Good for you for recognizing that something is wrong. It is unacceptable to exclude someone because of how they look. It's sizeism — prejudice or discrimination towards someone due to their size. Since this party is at your home, you can decide if those two people are invited. As for your friend, try turning the tables. Ask them how they would feel if they were not included because of their appearance.

Q: I have never had to worry about how I look. I guess it's natural that my little sister looks up to me and is always looking for my approval. The other day she told me that she wished that she could be as pretty as me. She said she feels like she was the ugly sister. What can I do to help her look her best?

— **Big Sister Duty**

A: It's wonderful that your little sister looks up to you. She may see you as her role model! But a ton of responsibility comes with that. Do you want your sister to feel like she's not enough? Do you want her to feel that if she can't look like you, she is somehow failing you? Take a good look at how you talk about appearances, because she is listening. Make a point of not talking negatively about your body or the bodies of others. If you model behaviour that does not focus on physical appearance, you can help your sister and yourself see that how you look is actually not that important. And if you ever are concerned about how your sister is feeling, be sure to let a trusted adult know.

HOW IS IT AFFECTING ME?

You may be influential to your peers, but how does this affect you? Is it helpful or harmful? Of the statements below, how many are true for you and how many are false? If you answered TRUE to more than ten of these statements, body image could be causing issues for you when you deal with other people. Consider speaking to someone about how you are feeling and how these beliefs are causing conflict.

1. I work hard at keeping up my physical appearance.
2. I worry about what others think of me.
3. I am terrified about my appearance changing.
4. I am critical about my body.
5. I am selective about what I eat.
6. My role models are all people I aspire to look like.
7. If I don't get compliments about how I look, I feel like I'm doing something wrong.
8. I exercise only to make sure I look good.
9. I make fun of people who are comfortable looking less than great.
10. I don't have many hobbies.
11. I feel pressure to maintain how I look.
12. I often have negative thoughts about myself and my body.
13. Most of my friends look like me.
14. I believe that looking good will get me far in life.
15. I sometimes wonder if my friends would still like me if I didn't look the way I do.

16. I am not as confident as I look.
17. I don't go out in public without wearing makeup.
18. I think people are only attracted to me because of how I look.
19. I don't step in when my friends make fun of others' appearance.
20. Gaining weight is the worst thing that could happen to me.
21. Getting likes and praise on social media can make my entire day.

22. I feel like most people do not know the real me.

23. I judge people based on what they look like.

24. I have a hard time concentrating on other tasks because I am always focused on how I look.

25. I want people to admire me.

26. Boys who have muscular bodies are good at everything.

27. It's important for girls to be attractive.

28. I spend endless hours on social media admiring people that I want to look like.

29. I don't understand people who don't care about what they look like.

30. I believe that ads and commercials tell the truth.

TAKE TIME FOR YOU!

The problem with being an influencer is that sometimes you're too busy to step back and figure out what you really feel. Here are some things you can do to find out what's important to you.

Reflect on your appearance. What thoughts or feelings come to mind when you think about the way you look? Are there beliefs you have about your appearance that cause you a lot of stress or prevent you from accepting yourself?

Explore your identity. Apart from your physical appearance, who are you? Write a list of ten things you like doing and skills you are most proud of. Take the time to discover who you are on the inside and do the things you enjoy.

Observe others. What thoughts come to mind when you see people of different shapes, heights, and sizes? Do you make judgements about their character based on their appearance? Do you assume groups of people have particular personalities or certain abilities based on their body type?

Observe yourself. Are you letting inaccurate stereotypes determine how you treat people? Assumptions about appearance can make you discriminate against others. It is important not to judge a person based on appearance. Take the time to get to know people who do not look like you.

Take care of yourself. We have our bodies for our entire lives. It is our responsibility to provide our bodies with love and care. Create a list of ten things you can do to take care of yourself. Whenever you are feeling down on yourself, check your list and show your body a little love.

Talk it out. Speak with an adult you trust if you are concerned about your body image and how it affects your life. Let them know exactly how you are feeling. Rather than bottling up your thoughts and feelings, it can be helpful to get some support and guidance.

DOs & DON'Ts

✓ Do recognize that you are worth more than your appearance.

✓ Do see that others are worth more than their appearance.

✓ Do take time to discover what you like about yourself apart from how you look.

✓ Do understand that beauty and attraction mean different things to different people.

✓ Do choose friends who add value to your life, not just friends who have the right look.

✓ Do put yourself in someone else's shoes.

✗ Don't judge others based on how they look.

✗ Don't treat others poorly because of their appearance.

✗ Don't support friends who treat others poorly because of their appearance.

✗ Don't get caught up in always trying to look good.

✗ Don't allow the media to tell you how you should look.

✗ Don't reinforce gender stereotypes.

DID YOU KNOW?

- On average, we use social media 144 minutes per day. For some, this number is even higher.

- We come across around 5,000 ads per day. Think about how many of these ads focus on physical appearance.

- The average person takes approximately 12 selfies before they post one online.

ARE YOU A WITNESS?

Ever caught a friend putting themselves down? Have you come across someone being bullied or teased about their physical appearance? What was your response?

Did you say or do anything when you saw something that was wrong? Well, why not?

Make the right choice.

When we see something happen that we know is not right, we have two options: stay silent or speak up. We may choose to remain silent because it feels comfortable or because we do not know what to do or say. These are valid reasons.

Supporting others looks good.

Just don't forget that your voice is powerful. When you see someone being mistreated, or when you're concerned about another person's well-being, speaking up is important and can help in many ways. Sometimes all it takes is one person speaking up to make a difference.

DOs & DON'Ts

✓ **Do realize that you can make a difference.**

✓ **Do speak up if you hear someone you know put themselves down.**

✓ **Do speak up if you hear someone you know put someone else down.**

✓ **Do let a friend or family member know if you are ever concerned about them.**

✓ **Do encourage others to seek help.**

✓ **Do talk to a trusted adult if you are unsure of what to do.**

✗ **Don't forget you can choose to speak up or to remain silent.**

✗ **Don't forget you can always ask for help.**

✗ **Don't be a part of the problem.**

✗ **Don't support people who show disrespect to others.**

✗ **Don't forget that you are capable of helping others.**

✗ **Don't think that you must handle any situation on your own.**

WHAT WOULD YOU DO?

Body image can be a touchy subject. It can be challenging to stand up or know what to do in conflicts related to something so personal. But it is important to remember that there are always options! On the next few pages you will find ten different scenarios and possible ways of dealing with them. No answer is right or wrong. You might even come up with a different solution that works for you!

1. Birthday Girl

You are at a friend's birthday party. The birthday girl asks everyone to come together for a group photo to post on social media. For the pic, she leads you to stand in front and tells Bryan, a classmate who is often teased because of his appearance, to stand in the back behind everyone else. Do you. . .

- Take your place and say nothing. It's your friend's party and social media feed.
- Offer to switch spots with Bryan.
- Suggest that pictures of small groups of people might be better than one big photo where some people could get left out.
- Take pictures of everyone to put on your own social media feed.
- Ask your friend why she told Bryan to stand in the back.
- Tell your friend that if she doesn't want everyone showing up in the photo, you don't want to be in the picture.

2. Locker Room Talk

You're in the change room and overhear two of your teammates chatting about girls at school. They are naming girls they would not date because of their weight, because of how much they have developed, or because of their facial features. They start mocking these girls and laughing. They ask you what you think. Do you. . .

- Tell them you haven't thought about the girls they are talking about.
- Say nothing.
- Ask them if they would date one of the girls for her great sense of humour, or another for her mad gaming skills.
- Remind them that just because they do not think a girl is attractive does not mean that she is not attractive.
- Notify a teacher or coach if you are concerned about sexism or bullying.

28

3. Photo Finish

Your friend posts a picture on social media. You recognize the picture as one you took. When you compare the two, you notice her skin appears to be much lighter than usual in the picture she posted. Do you...

- Let it go. It's up to your friend to decide how she wants to appear on her social media.
- Ask her why she edited the photo.
- Share with her examples of other beautiful women who look like her.
- If you notice other changes in your friend that make you think she is being too hard on herself, speak to a trusted adult.

4. Recess Response

During recess, a bully at your school teases your classmate about their weight. You can tell that your classmate is about to start crying. You know that will make the bullying even more vicious. Do you...

- Not get involved. Saying something might make the bully turn on you.
- Get your classmate away from the bully.
- Stick up for your classmate.
- Tell a teacher about the bullying.

5. Sleepover Dilemma

While at a weekend sleepover party, you notice one of your friends is eating more than usual. Then she disappears into the bathroom. When she is with you at the party, she seems to have something on her mind. She is quieter than usual. Do you...

- Say nothing, but plan to talk to your friend after the party.
- Find a private place to talk and ask your friend if everything is okay.
- Pull your friend aside and tell them what you have been noticing.
- Offer to go with your friend to speak to a trusted adult about what is happening.
- Let an adult know what is happening and that you're concerned.

6. Working Out

Your friend told you about an exercise routine they've been doing. You're worried because it sounds very extreme and your friend thinks it can help them lose a lot of weight really fast. Do you. . .

- Tell your friend you are concerned about the exercise routine and about their health.
- Remind your friend that exercise should be done in moderation and is meant to celebrate what our bodies can do, not torture them.
- Encourage your friend to talk about their exercise routine with their doctor.
- Let a trusted adult know what is happening and ask for help.

7. Change Room Challenge

You are out shopping with your friends and one goes into the change room to try on some clothes. While waiting, you hear sobbing coming from inside the change room. When you call out and ask your friend if everything is okay, she says that "nothing fits her." Do you. . .

- Ask if you can come in the change room to talk with her.
- Listen to what your friend has to say.
- Remind your friend that they are just clothes. If these clothes don't fit, there are other clothes that will.
- Suggest trying a different store.
- Tell your friend that her clothing size does not define her value.

8. Boyfriend Blues

Your older sister tells you that she doesn't feel good about herself and her body when she's around her boyfriend. He wants her to wear revealing clothes and makes comments about the parts of her body that he doesn't like. Do you. . .

- Stay out of it. Your sister might resent anything you say against her boyfriend.
- Remind your sister of the qualities you like about her. Tell her she should be around people who make her feel good.
- Ask your sister if she feels pressured to do anything drastic about changing her looks.
- Let a parent or guardian know what is happening.

9. Tall Story

Your basketball teammate uploads a photo of herself on social media. Someone leaves a comment underneath her photo saying, "How tall are you? You look like a giraffe." Do you. . .

- Laugh it off. Remind your teammate that there will always be trolls on social media.
- Encourage your teammate to delete the comment and block that person.
- Report the comment.

10. Fall Friend

You didn't see your friend all summer, so you make plans to get together. At the last minute, your friend cancels the hangout. When you ask why, they tell you they have gained a lot of weight and do not want to leave their home. Do you. . .

- Remind your friend that their weight has nothing to do with who they are or why you are friends.
- Ask if they would feel more comfortable meeting somewhere without a lot of people.
- Offer to come to them. Tell them that whether or not they've gained weight, their friends would like to see them.
- Let a trusted adult know if you're concerned that your friend is cutting themselves off from other parts of their life.

MORE HELP

If you or someone that you know is struggling with body image, know that there is help available and that you are not alone.

Helplines

Kids Help Phone 1-800-668-6868 or text 686868
First Nations and Inuit Hope for Wellness 1-855-242-3310
National Eating Disorder Information Centre (NEDIC) Helpline
1-866-NEDIC-20 and 416-340-4156
Black Youth Helpline 1-833-294-8650
The Trevor Project 1-866-488-7386
ConnexOntario Mental Health Helpline 1-866-531-2600
Canada Suicide Prevention Service (CSPS) 1-833-456-4566

Websites

National Eating Disorder Information Centre (NEDIC): www.nedic.ca
Body Brave: www.bodybrave.ca
Media Smarts:
www.mediasmarts.ca/body-image/media-education-and-body-image
Dove Self-Esteem Project: www.dove.com/ca/en/dove-self-esteem-project.html
Kids Help Phone: www.kidshelpphone.ca

Books

Under Our Clothes: Our First Talk About Our Bodies by Jillian Roberts. Orca Book Publishers, 2019.
Body Talk: The Straight Facts on Fitness, Nutrition, and Feeling Great About Yourself!: A Girl Zone Book by Ann Douglas, Julie Douglas, and Claudia Davila. Maple Tree Press, 2006.
Jammer Star by Kate Hargreaves. Orca Book Publishers, 2019.

More Deal With It Titles

Islamophobia by Safia Saleh, illustrated by Hana Shafi. Lorimer, 2020.
Consent by Keisha Evans and N. B. Gonsalvez, illustrated by Jenny Chan. Lorimer, 2020.
Freedom of Expression by Danielle S. McLaughlin, illustrated by Paris Alleyne. Lorimer, 2019.
Guyness by Steve Pitt, illustrated by Steven Murray. Lorimer, 2017.
Image by Kat Mototsune, illustrated by Ben Shannon. Lorimer, 2017.
Transphobia by j wallace skelton, illustrated by Nick Johnson. Lorimer, 2016.
Homophobia by Steven Solomon, illustrated by Nick Johnson. Lorimer, 2013.
Racism by Anne Marie Aikins, illustrated by Steven Murray. Lorimer, 2010.

Text Copyright © 2021 by Tierra Hohn
Illustration Copyright © 2021 James Lorimer & Company
Published in Canada in 2021. Published in the United States in 2021.

James Lorimer & Company Ltd., Publishers acknowledges funding support from the Ontario Arts Council (OAC), an agency of the Government of Ontario. We acknowledge the support of the Canada Council for the Arts, which last year invested $153 million to bring the arts to Canadians throughout the country. This project has been made possible in part by the Government of Canada and with the support of Ontario Creates.

Cover image: Shutterstock
Cover design: Tyler Cleroux
Series design: Tyler Cleroux

Library and Archives Canada Cataloguing in Publication

Title: Body image : deal with it because all bodies are great bodies / Tierra Hohn ; illustrated by Marne Grahlman.
Names: Hohn, Tierra, author. | Grahlman, Marne, illustrator.
Series: Deal with it (Toronto, Ont.)
Description: Series statement: Deal with it | Includes bibliographical references.
Identifiers: Canadiana 20200348604 | ISBN 9781459414532 (hardcover)
Subjects: LCSH: Body image in children—Juvenile literature. | LCSH: Body image—Juvenile literature. | LCSH: Body image disturbance—Juvenile literature. | LCSH: Self-esteem in children—Juvenile literature. | LCSH: Self-esteem—Juvenile literature. | LCSH: Self-perception in children—Juvenile literature. | LCSH: Self-perception—Juvenile literature.
Classification: LCC BF723.B6 H64 2021 | DDC j306.4/613—dc23

James Lorimer & Company Ltd., Publishers
117 Peter Street, Suite 304
Toronto, ON, Canada, M5V 0M3
www.lorimer.ca

Distributed in Canada by:
Formac Lorimer Books
5502 Atlantic Street
Halifax, NS, Canada
B3H 1G4
www.formaclorimerbooks.ca

Distributed in the US by:
Lerner Publisher Services
241 1st Ave. N.
Minneapolis, MN, USA
55401
www.lernerbooks.com

Printed and bound in Korea.